Kitchen Math

Miguel Rosario

Cavendish
Square
New York

Published in 2015 by Cavendish Square Publishing, LLC
243 5th Avenue, Suite 136, New York, NY 10016

Copyright © 2015 by Cavendish Square Publishing, LLC

First Edition

Library of Congress Cataloging-in-Publication Data

Rosario, Miguel, author.
Kitchen math / Miguel Rosario.
pages cm. — (Math around us)
Includes index.
ISBN 978-1-50260-157-5 (hardcover) ISBN 978-1-50260-160-5 (paperback) ISBN 978-1-50260-163-6 (ebook)
1. Counting—Juvenile literature. 2. Mathematics—Juvenile literature. 3. Cooking—Juvenile literature. I. Title.

QA113.R6715 2015
513.2—dc23

2014032625

Editor: Amy Hayes
Copy Editor: Cynthia Roby
Art Director: Jeffrey Talbot
Designer: Douglas Brooks
Senior Production Manager: Jennifer Ryder-Talbot
Production Editor: David McNamara
Photo Researcher: J8 Media

The photographs in this book are used by permission and through the courtesy of: Cover photo by Dave & Les Jacobs/Getty Images; andresr/E+/Getty Images, 5; Blend Images/John Lund/Marc Romanelli/Getty Images, 7; Blend Images/John Lund/Marc Romanelli/Vetta/Getty Images, 9; Oksana Kuzmina/Shutterstock.com, 11; © iStockphoto.com/p_ponomareva, 13; Eric Audras/ONOKY/Getty Images, 15; © iStockphoto.com/AVAVA, 17; Fuse/Getty Images, 19; JGI/Jamie Grill/Blend Images/Getty Images, 21.

Printed in the United States of America

Contents

Math in the Kitchen 4

New Words 22

Index 23

About the Author 24

Cooking in the kitchen is fun!

How many people are in this kitchen?

3 people are in this kitchen.

4

5

Martha washes her hands before she helps in the kitchen.

How many hands does Martha wash?

Martha washes **2** hands.

7

Nick and his dad cut up a watermelon.

First they cut **5** pieces, and then they cut **3** more.

How many pieces of watermelon were cut?

8 pieces of watermelon were cut.

Jenna and her mother cut **3** peppers and **2** tomatoes.

How many **vegetables** did they cut?

They cut **5** vegetables.

Matt and his dad make
a **salad**.

How many people make
a salad?

2 people make a salad.

Danny and his dad bake bread.

How many **loaves** of bread do you see?

There are **2** loaves of bread.

Lana and Emily have **12** eggs.

They crack **2** eggs.

How many eggs are left?
10 eggs are left.

Kayla and her mom **measure** sugar.

Kayla measures **1** cup, then **2** more.

How many cups of sugar does Kayla measure?

Kayla measures **3** cups.

18

19

How many balls of cookie **dough** do you see?

There are **9** balls of cookie dough.

Kitchen math sure is tasty!

New Words

dough (DOE) A soft mass of wet flour or meal thick enough to knead or roll.

loaves (LOWVS) Shaped or molded pieces of bread.

measure (MEH-sure) To find out how much there is of something.

salad (SAL-ad) A mixture of food, usually fruits or vegetables.

vegetables (VEJ-tah-bulz) Plants grown from the ground that you eat.

Index

dough, 20

eggs, 16

hands, 6

loaves, 14

measure, 18

people, 4, 12

salad, 12

vegetables, 10

watermelon, 8

About the Author

Miguel Rosario lives in Ellicottville, New York. He has two beautiful daughters and a great big dog named Elmo.

About

Bookworms help independent readers gain reading confidence through high-frequency words, simple sentences, and strong picture/text support. Each book explores a concept that helps children relate what they read to the world they live in.